Old Time Bottles

Found in the Ghost Towns

by Lynn Blumenstein
Author of
"REDIGGING THE WEST"
"BOTTLE RUSH U.S.A."
"WISHBOOK 1865"

Pictures and prices of over 300 bottles in the 50 to over 100 year class that are to be found in Ghost Towns of the west.

Published by
OLD TIME BOTTLE PUBLISHING CO.
Salem, Oregon

INTRODUCTION

1634756

This book is meant to acquaint one with the fascinating hobby of bottle collecting in the "Ghost Towns" of the west, also hints in regard to how and where to obtain bottles from these areas.

There has always been mystery and wonderment concerning the people and their habits, who lived in the wild and wooley mining towns of the eighteen hundreds. In searching through the rubble of these towns, a great deal of information can be gathered. For example; it has been revealed that the placer miner of years ago was generally a moderate drinker and lived mostly out of the can. In contrast, his brother gold seeker, the hardrock miner consumed large amounts of varied alcoholic beverages and was forever troubled with poor digestion from his rather limited diet.

In the camps of the miners, who came later in the search for gold, a great abundance of extract bottles have been uncovered in the frenzied search for bottles of the past. At first this was a mystery; however, it became apparent that this was the era of prohibition and that the contents of the extract bottle were being used for purposes other than what it had been originally intended. It also has been noted that lemon extract was undoubtedly the favorite.

Some of the many pleasures derived from bottle collecting is that you very seldom come home empty-handed and all old bottles will bring a price. In fact, some, a very handsome profit from certain collectors.

Another of the many rewards is to get away from the hustle and bustle of our now busy cities and roam about the long forgotten towns of the past, with their weathered buildings, empty, silent, and worn thresholds, now covered with dust, where the restless tread of youth and dreams passed, laughter, loud voices, the creak of wagons; raw lusty living, now a mute reminder of a time forever past.

BOTTLE HISTORY

At the start of the gold rush in 1849, the miners poured into the west by the thousands, with the miner came his bottles. As soon as camps and towns were erected, a flow of liquor, remedy, and all sorts of household bottles started their long journey first by ship, then by wagon, to the prosperous mining towns.

Nearly all of the old bottles were of a cork type. There, also, were many bottles made that look a great deal like our present type bottle; however, they were a cork type bottle with a wire clamp holding down the cork. The glass that was used in making some of the old bottles, was often made with an impure silica, hence allowing the glass to color when left out in the sun for some time.

Whenever you are trying to determine old bottles from new bottles you should look for bubbles, crevices, imperfections, such as uneven bottoms, crooked necks, and scratches made by wooden molds.

BITTERS ERA

The Bitters era was one of particular interest because of the wide variety of bottles manufactured. Bitters originated in England and soon became popular in the United States. They were made in a wide variety in hope that they would be kept for other uses, and hence would further advertise the producet. The Bitters were noted to cure almost anything, as: kidney, liver, bladder disease, pimples, indigestion, fever, malaria, etc.

THE SEARCH

In the search for bottles it would be best to become acquainted with the history of the particular area of interest. This can be done very easily by inquiring at City and State libraries. It is also advantageous to visit museums, bottle shops and antique stores. The actual search and excavating for bottles is very similar to the methods used in mining. With this information and with the knowledge of the habits of the people, the way has been facilitated toward making a good find.

City dumps of the Ghost Towns, generally are found in heavily wooded sections, because it offered protection to livestock, serving the purpose as a fence. Most often the glass in city dumps was discarded at the base of a large tree, the reason being; that if you walked around the tree, you walked around the glass. Sometimes bottles were placed in gunnysacks that hung in the woodsheds at which time they were purposely broken so that the sack would hold more. Whereever the remains were dumped, piles of broken glass are found.

In searching for bottles there are areas where nothing but tin cans are found. It becomes evident that the glass has been separated and buried elsewhere, generally in a small pit. There would be a layer of glass and garbage placed, then a layer of dirt and so on until the pit was filled and covered over. Wherever these pits are found it can be assured that a woman was present, as the pit served two purposes; it kept the glass away from the children's feet and discouraged animals from lurking near the cabin.

In contrast to the home where the woman abided with her family, the bachelor's life brings an entirely different story. This individual used no particular system in discarding his refuse. If he had a system it was whichever place was convenient at the moment. He threw his debris out of windows, doors, and in the front and back yards. Another favorite place where bottles are found in is the old outhouses. It appears that whenever a trip was made in that direction, a load of garbage also went out!

Creek banks are probably the most favored places in which to search for bottles. Whenever a creek is located near any place of inhabitants this is where the refuse will be found. In some cases the water has washed away many good finds; however, there generally will be plenty to dig, on or near the creek banks.

The experienced collector searches for bottles, as the old miner did in exploring for gold. The collector looks for small thick pieces of glass, parts of dishes, tin cans, ironware, bones, etc.; he traces these items in hope that they might reveal a dump. Whenever any amount of refuse is found he immediately finds the depth of the dump and then follows its course. If he runs out of debris, he backs up and proceeds in another direction hoping to pick up another trace, his manner of procedure corresponds to the miner.

Another mining method that has been used is the system of hydraulic mining. This method can be applied whenever water is readily available. The equipment needed is a small motor, and a pump with a fair amount of fire, hose, accompanied with a high pressure nozzle, then place this equipment near a body of water. A trench must be dug to the very bottom of the debris, also, a path is dug for the used water to flow away. Then proceed to cut away the bank of refuse with the water from the hose.

Occasionally boulders and dirt will have to be pitched and shoveled away, because they may accumulate faster than the water can remove them. One nice factor about this method is that it is cool work and the bottles become partially cleaned.

A word of caution is made whenever mining methods are used, such as digging to great depth in an old well. Many times refuse was thrown in after the well became contaminated and the dangerous hole was filled to prevent accidents. These shafts must be shored with timbers or a person could very well be trapped or killed by a cave in or falling debris from above.

GOLD DREDGE

OLD HOSPITAL

DEATH OF A TOWN

MINER'S CABIN

HOTEL

SALOON, DRUG STORE & COURT HOUSE

MAIN STREET

STILL REMAINING

FALSE FRONT STORE

HIGH ON A MOUNTAIN SIDE WITH THE FOG ROLLING IN.

GONE IS THE MINER

GONE IS THE MINER —

Rambling through this old Ghost Town
Brings memories of the miner,
Bustling and churning with life
In the days of the forty-niner.

For pleasure he gambled and drank
With a sandpaper leathery skin;
He was a robust hearty worker
And wiped sweat from his whiskered chin.

The miner left his enduring mark
Of his hard and toilsome day,
Remnants of his hand-hewed cabin
Stands deteriorating away.

Now a tumble-weed rolls and rolls
With a wind swirling gust,
It is the only thing stirring
On this deserted road of dust.

The miner's gone, and with him
Went his life of the past,
All that remains behind
Are memories that last and last.

BJB

Left to Right

Historical Flask **Shield with five stripes** **& thirteen stars; over** **100 years old.** **Color Aqua**	Price is Open
Whiskey Flask **Color Amber**	$6.00 - $8.00
Whiskey Flask **Color Amber**	$8.00 - $10.00
Picnic Flask **Amethyst**	$3.50 - $6.00
Picnic Flask **Color Amethyst**	$4.00 - $6.00

Left to Right

Whiskey Color Amethyst	$5.00 - $6.00
Liquor Color Amber	$1.50 - $2.50
Liquor Color Amber	$1.50 - $3.00
Mineral Water Saxlehner's Bitterquelle Hunyadi Janos Color Olive Green	$4.00 - $6.00

Left to Right

Beer **Color Amber**	$2.00 - $2.50
Beer **Color Aqua**	$1.00 - $1.50
Whiskey **Color Amber**	$2.50 - $3.00
Whiskey **Color Amethyst**	$1.00 - $2.00

Left to Right

Beer
Color Aqua

$1.00 - $1.50

Brandy
Color Amber

$2.00 - $2.50

Lion Brewery LTD.
Reg. Trade Mark
Auckland Lion
Ale & Stout
Color Amber

$4.00 - $6.00

Left to Right

Whiskey **Color Amber**	$3.00 - $3.50
Sunny Brook The Pure Food Whiskey **Seals Read (Grand Prize St. Louis 1904)** **(Gold Medal St. Louis 1904)** **Color Clear** **Gold Lettering**	$12.00 - $18.00
Reproduction of the famous **E. G. Booz bottle** **1840** **Color Amber**	If original - would be over $300.00
Decantor **Color Amethyst**	$10.00 - $14.00

Left to Right

Whiskey $3.50 - $6.00
Dallemand & Co. Inc.
Chicago
Color Amber

Brandy $4.00 - $5.00
Color Amethyst

Kellogg's $24.00 - $32.00
Nelson County
Extra Kentucky
Bourbon Whiskey
W. L. Co.
Sole Agent
Screw threads
inside of neck
Color Amber

Brandy $22.00 - $24.00
Color Red Amber

Left to Right

JUG **Color Brown Top**	$4.00 - $6.00
JUG **Color Brown Top**	$4.00 - $5.00
JUG **Color Brown Top**	$6.00 - $8.00

Left to Right

Syrup Armour & Co. Chicgo Color Yellow	$5.00 - $7.00
Barber Shop Bottle Color Amber	$50.00 - $60.00
Chinese Win Jug Color Amber	$3.00 - $4.00
Pottery Bottle Color Brick Red	$ .50 - $ .75

Left to Right

K. C. B. & Co.
Color Amber
$1.50 - $2.50

Wine
Color Aqua
$1.00 to $2.00

American Brewing
& C I Co.
Baker City Ore.
Color Amber
$3.00 - $4.00

Whiskey
Color Amethyst
$1.50 - $2.00

Left to Right

California Punch Color Amber	$2.00 - $2.50
Whiskey Color Green	$2.00 - $3.00
Whiskey Color Clear	$1.00 - $2.00
Pabst Beer Color Dark Amber	$2.00 - $2.50
Pabst Beer Neck Label reads Premium Award Paris Exposition 1878 Color Amber	$3.00 - $4.50

Left to Right

Cosmetic Type **Color Amethyst**	$1.50 - $2.00
Lorrimer **Medical Institute** **Baltimore, MD.** **Color Amber**	$2.00 - $2.75
Acid **Color Aqua**	$ .75 - $1.00
Medical **Color Amber**	$ .50 - $ .75
Medical **Color Amber**	$1.00 - $1.50

Left to Right

6 oz. Mart T Goldman St. Paul Minn. Color Amber	$3.00 - $3.50
Rubifoam For the Teeth Color Clear	$2.00 - $2.50
Pa-Pay-Ans Bell Color Amber	$2.50 - $3.00
Listerine Color Clear	$ .50 - $ .75
Doct Marshall's Catarrh Snuff Color Aqua	$3.00 - $3.50
Hall's Catarrh Cure Color Clear	$2.00 - $3.50

Left to Right

Brandy **Color Amethyst**	$1.50 - $2.50
Brandy **Color Amethyst**	$1.50 - $2.50
Brandy **Color Amethyst**	$1.50 - $2.50

Left to Right

Kellogg's Co. Wilmerding - Loewe San Francisco Color Amber	$14.00 - $18.00
Whiskey (3-piece mold) Color Amber	$3.00 - $4.00
Pluto Water American Physic Pictures of Pluto on bottom Color Aqua	$1.00 - $1.50
Whiskey Full Quart Color Amber	$3.00 - $6.00

Left to Right

WINE **Color Green**	$1.00 - $2.00
CHAMPAGNE **Color Green**	$ .75 - $1.25
CHAMPAGNE **Color Green**	$ .75 - $1.50
WINE **Color Green**	$1.00 - $2.50
WINE **Color Amethyst**	$1.00 - $2.50

Left to Right

Lash's Kidney & Liver Bitters Color Amber	$8.00 - $9.00
Dr. S. B. H. Co. PR. Color Aqua	$2.00 - $3.00
Hoods Sarsa Parilla Color Aqua	$5.00 - $6.00
The Great Dr. Kilmers Swamp Root, Kidney, Liver & Bladder Remedy Color Aqua	$6.00 - $8.00
Dr. Kilmers Swamp Root, Kidney, Liver & Bladder Remedy Color Aqua	$5.00 - $7.00
Dr. J. Hostetters Stomach Bitters Color Amber	$4.00 - $5.00

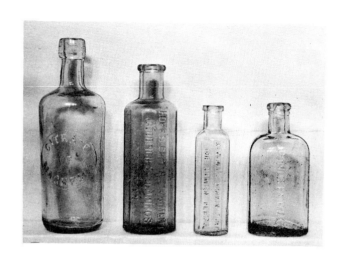

Left to Right

Citrate of Magnesia $1.00 - $2.00
Color Amethyst

Hoff's German Liniment $2.50 - $3.50
Goodrich & Jennings
Anoka, Minn.
Twelve Sided
Color Amethyst

Kendall's Spavin Cure $3.00 - $3.50
for Human Flesh
Ten Sided
Color Aqua

Ponds Extract $1.00 - $2.00
1846
Color Aqua

Left to Right

Shoo-Fly Flask Color Aqua	$3.50 - $4.00
The Piso Co. Color Emerald	$2.00 - $2.50
Dr. D. Jayne's **Tonic Vermifuge** Color Aqua	$1.50 - $2.00
J. E. Combault's **Caustic Balsam** Color Aqua	$2.00 - $3.00
Ayer's **Cherry Pectoral** Color Aqua	$1.50 - $2.00
Davis Painkiller Color Aqua	$1.50 - $3.00

Left to Right

Seasoning Bottle **Color Green**	**$3.50 - $4.00**
Shillings **S. A. & Co.** **Color Amethyst**	**$1.00 - $1.50**
WM. R. Warner Co. **Philadelphia** **New** **Chicago** **Color Clear**	**$ .50 - $ .75**
Shillings **S. B. & Co.** **Color Amethyst**	**$1.00 - $1.50**
Shillings **S. B. & Co.** **Color Amethyst**	**$1.00 - $1.50**
Buckeye **Olympia, Wash.** **Color Amethyst**	**$1.50 - $2.50**

Left to Right

Peppers **Color Green**	$3.50 - $5.00
Green Peppers in Vinegar Sauce **Color Clear**	$9.00 - $10.00
Dodson Hills **St. Louis** **Color Clear**	$1.25 - $1.50
Olive Oil **Picture of Bird on Bottom** **Color Aqua**	$1.25 - $1.50
Olive Oil **Color Clear**	$2.00 - $2.50
Olive Oil **Color Clear**	$1.50 - $2.00

Left to Right

Purola **Color Amethyst**	$ .50 - $1.00
J. A. Folger & Co **San Francisco** **Kansas City** **Color Clear**	$ .75 - $1.00
Foley & Co. **Color Clear**	$ .75 - $1.00
Dr. Kings New Discovery **For Consumption** **Color Aqua**	$2.00 - $3.00
Dr. Kings New Discovery **for Coughs and Colds** **Color Clear**	$2.00 - $3.00
Scotts Emulsion **Cod Liver Oil** **Color Aqua**	$1.50 - $3.00

Left to Right

Three in One Oil **Color Aqua**	$1.00 - $1.25
Three in One Oil **Color Aqua**	$1.00 - $1.25
Hires Root Beer **Makes Five Gallons of** **a Delicious Drink** **Color Aqua**	$2.00 - $2.50
Extract **Color Amethyst**	$ .50 - $ .75
National Remedy Co. **New York** **Color Clear**	$ .50 - $1.00

Left to Right

Chamberlain's Pain Balm
Color Aqua

1634756

$1.50 - $2.50

Folger's Golden Gate Flavoring
Color Clear

$1.00 - $2.00

Extract 2 oz. Full Measure
Color Clear

$ .50 - $ .75

The Northrop & Sturgis Co.
Flavoring Extracts
Color Clear

$1.50 - $2.50

Hamlins Wizard Oil
Color Aqua

$1.50 - $2.50

Dr. Prices Delicious Flavoring Extracts
Color Clear

$2.00 - $2.50

Left to Right

Chas. F. H. Fletcher **Castoria** **Color Aqua**	**$1.00 - $2.00**
E. C. Dewitt & Co. **Color Aqua**	**$1.50 - $2.00**
California Fig Syrup **Color Clear**	**$1.50 - $2.50**
Caldwell's Syrup Pepsin **Color Aqua**	**$2.00 - $3.50**
Medical **Heavy Glass** **Color Aqua**	**$1.50 - $2.00**

Left to Right

K. B. Heavy Glass Eight Sided Color Emerald	$2.50 - $3.00
Preserve Type Color Clear	$5.00 - $6.50
Prserve Type Color Clear	$1.50 - $2.00
Preserve Type Color Aqua	$1.00 - $2.00

Left to Right

Pickles or Olives Color Amethyst	$1.50 - $2.50
Preserve Type Color Amethyst	$ .75 - $1.00
Preserve Type Color Amethyst	$ .75 - $1.00
Preserve Type Color Amethyst	$ .75 - $1.25

Left to Right

Mission Dry Orange **Color Black** **(deep purple)**	$3.00 - $4.00
Beer **Color Aqua**	$ .50 - $ .75
Beer **Color Aqua**	$ .75 - $1.00
Beer **Color Amber**	$1.00 - $1.50

Left to Right

Catsup Color Clear	$ .50 - $ .75
Catsup Color Clear	$ .75 - $1.00
Preferred Stock Catsup Extra Quality Color Amethyst	$ .75 - $1.25
Reifs Special Color Amber	$1.00 - $2.50
Catsup The T. A. Snider Preserve Co. Cincinnati, O. Color Amethyst	$1.00 - $1.50

Left to Right

Sauce Bottle Color Clear	$3.00 - $3.50
Mustard Color Amethyst	$1.50 - $2.00
Mustard Color Clear	$1.50 - $2.00
Horse Radish Color Aqua	$1.00 - $1.50
Chas. Gulden New York Color Clear	$2.00 - $3.00

Left to Right

Moutarde Diaphane Louit Freres & Co. Color Amethyst	$3.00 - $4.00
Chas. Gulden Color Amethyst	$1.00 - $1.50
Mustard Color Amethyst	$1.00 to $1.75
E. R. Durkee & Co. Color Clear	$1.00 - $1.75
E. R. Durkee & Co. Salad Dressing New York Color Clear	$1.00 - $1.75

Left to Right

H. J. Heinz Co. Color Aqua	$ .50 - $ .75
H. J. Heinz Co. Color Aqua	$ .50 - $ .75
Dodson Hills Mfg. Co. Color Aqua	$ .50 - $1.00
Dodson Hills Mfg. Co. Color Amethyst	$ .50 - $1.00
Relish Bottle Color Clear	$3.00 - $4.00

Left to Right

Horseradish **Mustard** **Geo A. Bayle** **Color Clear**	$3.50 - $4.50
Relish Bottle **Color Amethyst**	$3.00 - $4.00
Charles Gulden **New York** **Color Amethyst**	$1.00 - $2.00
H. J. Heinz Co. **Pat. June 9, 1891** **Ten Sided** **Color Amethyst**	$1.00 - $1.50
Olive Bottle **Color Clear**	$ .75 - $1.00

Left to Right

H. J. Heinz Co. **Color Aqua**	$1.00 - $1.25
Chutney **Color Amethyst**	$1.50 - $2.50
Chutney **Color Aqua**	$3.00 - $4.00
Pickle **Color Clear**	$3.50 - $4.50

Left to Right

Olive Bottle **Color Clear**	$ .50 - $ .75
Olive Bottle **Color Clear**	$ .50 - $ .75
Olive Bottle **Color Amethyst**	$ .50 - $ .75
Olive Bottle **Color Clear**	$3.00 - $4.00

Left to Right

BEER
Color Amber

$1.00 - $1.50

BEER
Color Amber

$1.50 - $2.00

BEER
Color Amber

$3.00 - $4.50

Left to Right

Beverage Color Jade	$3.00 - $4.00
Beverage (Chinese) Color Amber	$1.00 - $1.50
Wine Color Green	$1.00 - $1.50
Beverage Color Amber	$1.00 - $2.00

Left to Right

Standard Mason **Color Light Green**	$3.00 - $4.00
Mason's Pat. **Nov. 30, 1858** **Color Light Green**	$4.00 - $6.00
Root Mason **Color Light Green**	$4.00 - $5.00

Left to Right

Schram Automatic Sealer Color Amethyst	$5.00 - $6.00
Economy Everlasting Jar Color Amethyst	$3.00 - $4.00
Improved Everlasting Jar Color Amethyst	$10.00 - $12.00

Left to Right

JUG Color Amethyst	$2.50 - $3.50
JUG Color Amethyst	$2.00 - $3.00
MINERAL WATER Color Light Green	$2.50 - $3.50

Left to Right

Horlick's Original **Lunch Tablets** **Color Clear**	$2.00 - $3.00
Horlick's Malted Milk **Color Clear**	$2.00 - $2.50
Horlick's Malted Milk **Racine, Wis. U.S.A.** **London Eng.** **Color Light Green**	$3.00 - $5.00

Left to Right

Beverage Color Aqua	$ .75 - $1.00
Beverage Bottle Color Aqua	$1.50 - $2.50
Soda Water Property of Inland Coca Cola Co. Color Clear	$4.00 - $5.00
Raven Splits Color Amber	$2.00 - $2.50
E & J Burk Picture of Cat on Bottom with Five Dots Color Green	$2.50 - $3.00
Beverage Color Aqua	$2.50 - $3.50

Left to Right

BEER **Color Aqua**	$ .50 - $ .75
BEER **Color Aqua**	$ .50 - $ .75
BEER **Color Aqua**	$1.00 - $2.00
BEER **Light Blue**	$1.50 - $2.00

Left to Right

Lea & Perrins Worcestershire Sauce
Color Aqua

$ .75 - $1.00

Lea & Perrins Worcestershire Sauce
Color Aqua

$ .75 - $1.00

Sauce Bottle
Six-Sided
Color Amethyst

$4.50 - $6.00

Sauce Bottle
Color Blue

$2.00 - $3.00

Pepper Sauce
Color Amethyst

$3.50 - $5.00

Left to Right

Extract **J. A. F. & Co.** **Color Clear**	$1.00 - $1.25
Foley & Co. **Color Clear**	$ .75 - $1.00
Olive Oil **Color Amethyst**	$1.00 - $1.50
Mc Ilhenny **Tabasco Sauce** **Color Clear**	$ .50 - $1.00
Castor Oil **Color Aqua**	$1.00 - $1.50

Left to Right

INK BOTTLE Color Clear	$1.50 - $2.50
INK BOTTLE Color Amethyst	$4.00 - $4.50
INK BOTTLE Color Aqua	$1.50 - $2.50
INK BOTTLE Color Clear	$1.50 - $2.00
INK BOTTLE Color Aqua	$1.50 - $2.50
INK BOTTLE Color Aqua	$2.50 - $3.50

Left to Right

INK BOTTLE Color Dark Amber	$8.00 - $10.00
BOAT INK Color Aqua	$12.00 - $15.00
INK BOTTLE Color Light Blue	$2.50 - $3.00
INK BOTTLE Color Aqua	$8.00 - $9.50
UMBRELLA INK Color Aqua	$9.00 - $12.00
INK BOTTLE Color Aqua	$8.00 - $12.00

Left to Right

DeWitts Colic & Cholera Cure **Color Aqua**	$4.00 - $5.00
Chamberlain's Colic and **Diarrhea Remedy** **Color Aqua**	$2.00 - $3.00
Medical **Color Amethyst**	$ .50 - $ .75
Extract **Color Clear**	$ .50 - $ .75
Lemon Extract **Color Amethyst**	$ .50 - $ .75

Left to Right

MEDICAL Color Amethyst	$ .50 - $ .75
MEDICAL Color Amber	$1.00 - $1.50
MEDICAL Color Clear	$1.50 - $2.00
MEDICAL Color Amethyst	$ .50 - $ .75
MEDICAL Color Aqua	$ .75 - $1.00
MEDICAL Color Clear	$ .50 - $ .75
MEDICAL Color Clear	$ .50 - $ .75

Left to Right

Small Bottles **Colors Green, Aqua,** **Amethyst and Clear**	1 to 7 $3.50
8. **Chinese** **Opium Bottls** **Color Aqua**	$1.50 - $2.00
9. **Hoods Pills** **Coreliverills** **Dose 1 to 4** **Cihodg & Co.** **Lowell, Mass.** **U. S. A.** **Color Clear**	$3.00 - $3.50

Left to Right

Small Bottles **Colors Amethyst, Aqua** **Clear and Green**	1 to 7 $3.00
8. **Lazell Perfume** **Color Amethyst**	$1.50 - $2.00

9. **Murine Eye Remedy**
    Chicago U. S. A.
    Color Clear
	$1.00 - $1.50

Left to Right

Sumpter Drug Co. - L.C. Edwards Prop. **Sumpter, Ore.** **Color Clear**	$2.00 - $2.50
Sumpter Drug Co. - L.C. Edwards, Prop. **Sumpter, Ore.** **Color Clear**	$2.00 - $3.00
Muegge The Druggist - Baker, Ore. **Color Clear**	$2.00 - $2.50
Muegge The Druggist - Baker, Ore. **Color Clear**	$2.00 - $3.00
Muegge The Druggist - Baker, Ore. **Color Clear**	$3.00 - $3.50

Left to Right

MEDICAL **Color Amethyst**	**$1.00 - $1.50**
MEDICAL **Color Amber**	**$ .50 - $ .75**
Pompeian Massage Cream **Color Amethyst**	**$1.00 - $1.25**
MEDICAL **Color Amber**	**$ .50 - $ .75**
MEDICAL **Color Clear**	**$ .50 - $ .75**
LYSOL **Color Amber**	**$ .50 - $ .75**

Left to Right

A. S. Hinds Color Clear	$ .50 - $ .75
Gebhart Eagle Chili Powder Color Clear	$ .50 - $ .75
Gebhart Eagle Chili Powder Color Clear	$ .50 - $ .75
Chesebrough Manfg. Co. New York Color Clear	$ .50 - $ .75
Vaseline Color Clear	$1.00 - $1.50
Vaseline Color Amber	$ .50 - $1.00
Vaseline Color Amethyst	$ .50 - $ .75

Left to Right

Zemo Mfg. **E. W. Rose Co., Cleveland, O** **Color Clear**	$1.00 - $1.25
Bathroom Type **Color Clear**	$ .75 - $1.00
Frostilla **Color Amethyst**	$1.00 - $1.50
Mrs. Stewarts Bluing **Color Aqua**	$ .50 - $ .75
Sauce Bottle **Color Amber**	$10.00 - $12.00

Left to Right

Medical Color Amber	$ .75 - $1.00
Medical Color Amber	$ .50 - $ .75
Liquozone Color Amber	$ .50 - $ .75
Medical Color Amber	$ .50 - $ .75
Medical Color Amber	$ .50 - $ .75
Medical Color Amber	$1.00 - $1.50

Left to Right

Medical $ .50 - $ .75
Color Clear

Medical $ .50 - $ .75
Color Amber

Medical $ .50 - $ .75
Color Clear

Medical $ .75 - $1.00
Color Amber

Left to Right

76 Liniment **Color Clear**	$1.00 - $2.00
Medical **Color Amber**	$1.00 - $1.50
Medical **Color Aqua**	$1.00 - $1.50
Medical **Color Amber**	$ .50 - $ .75

Left to Right

Medical **Color Clear**	$ .50 - $ .75
WM. R. Warner & Co. **Philadelphia** **Color Cobalt Blue**	$1.50 - $2.00
Medical **Color Clear**	$ .50 - $ .75
Milk of Magnesia **Color Cobalt Blue**	$1.50 - $2.50
Beef Iron & Wine **Color Clear**	$2.50 - $3.00

Left to Right

Armour Laboratories
Chicago
Color Amber

$1.00 - $2.00

Bevricke Runyon Co.
Color Clear

$1.00 - $1.75

O. D. Chem. Co.
Color Amber

$1.00 - $2.00

Owl Drug
Color Amethyst

$3.50 - $4.00

Left to Right

Beverage Color Aqua	$6.00 - $6.50
Gold Leaf Shoe Polish Color Light Green	$ .75 - $1.00
Catsup Color Amethyst	$1.00 - $1.25
Barrel Mustard Color Lavender	$2.00 - $3.00
Relish Type Color Amethyst	$1.00 - $1.25

Left to Right

Milk of Magnesia **Color Cobalt Blue**	$ .75 - $1.00
Bromo Seltzer **Color Cobalt Blue**	$1.50 - $2.50
John Wyeth & Bro., Pat. May 16, 1899 **reads around neck** **"Take Next Dose At . . ."** **Color Cobalt Blue**	$7.00 - $9.00
Bromo Seltzer **Color Cobalt Blue**	$1.00 - $1.25
Medical **Color Cobalt Blue**	$ .75 - $1.25
Medical **Color Cobalt Blue**	$ .75 - $1.25
New Skin Co. **Color Cobalt Blue**	$1.50 - $2.00

Left to Right

Wine **Color Green**	$2.50 - $3.00
Welch's Grape Juice **Color Clear**	$ .75 - $1.00
J. Gund BR'G **La Crosse Wis.** **EST. 1854** **Color Aqua**	$2.00 - $2.50
Wine **Color Green**	$1.00 - $1.50
Beverage **Color Aqua**	$1.00 - $1.25

INDEX

OLD WATER WORKS

NOW SILENT

CLEANING OPALESCENT BOTTLES

Bottles that have been buried for many years deserve special handling when cleaning. Before washing always have the bottles at room temperature. Rinse off the soil that will come off under a gentle flow of tepid water from the tap. Set the bottles upon a newspaper, drip dry enough to view if the bottle shows any sign of opalescence (*an irridescent play of pearly colors as in an Opal*) created by Hydrous Silica, variously colored and often transparent. Opalescence may lay beneath a coating of Calcite (*a widely diffused calcium carbonate usually colorless or whitish*). If there are signs of opalescence in either color or design, handle with care.

Attempt to avoid handling the body of the bottle. Place a finger in the neck of the bottle and tip, placing your other hand under the bottom when lifting. To clean use a solution of sudsy amonia and tepid water; with a wad of cotton gently clean, but do not scrub! Clean the inside of the bottle as much as you dare without handling the bottle directly. Cleaning the inside of the bottle is not too important as the bottle should be displayed with the use of indirect lighting. When you have completed the cleaning of the bottle, rince in clear tepid water and set upon a paper to drip dry. Always set your bottles so that they have air space around them and the undesired outside coating will begin to flake off. In a few days try blowing upon the bottles and the flakes will fly like snow. When the flaking stops, set back into a light solution of amonia for a few minutes, remove, drip dry and nature takes its course.

Your opalescent bottles displayed with light shining upon them (not through them) will show all of their beautiful colors brilliantly. If the bottles have been scrubbed, the brilliance will be dulled when set upright.

Heavy opalescence is found on bottles that have been buried for a long period of time and are coated with nature's aesthetic design. The signs of age are the proof of our pioneer heritage. Clean your bottles but don't destroy their look of age.

(page 47, 3rd bottle on right)
O. T. B.

SUGGESTED PERIODICALS

The Association
Gene Ballinger
Treasure Bank Building
P. O. Box 412
Oscoda, Michigan 48750

True Treasure
John Latham
P. O. Drawer L
Conroe, Taxas 77301

The Gold Bug
Art Lassagne
P. O. Box 588
Alamo, California 94507

**The National Treasure Hunters
League** - Ray Smith
P. O. Box 53
Mesquite, Texas 75149

**The Prospectors Club
International** - Ernie Webb
P. O. Box 729
Odessa, Texas 97960

The National Bottle Gazette
John C. Fountain
Amador City, California 95601

Treasure & Ghost Town Maps
Jack Cubit
Route 2
Twin Falls, Idaho 83301

The American Barbwire Journal
P. O. Box 195
Snyder, Texas 79549

For other books on bottle collecting,

write for free illustrative brochure.

OLD TIME BOTTLE PUBLISHING COMPANY
Department L.
611 Lancaster Dr. N.E.
Salem, Oregon 97301

Phone:
Area Code 503
362-1446

3455